Presentation by *BookLeaf Publishing*

Web: www.bookleafpub.com

E-mail: info@bookleafpub.com

ISBN: 9789395223058

First edition 2023

Love Lessons

Kelsey Ferguson

BookLeaf
Publishing

India | USA | UK

*Thank you for helping me see who I am and
what I'm worth.*

Sun

The sun on my skin
Brings me back to the present.
Making memories.

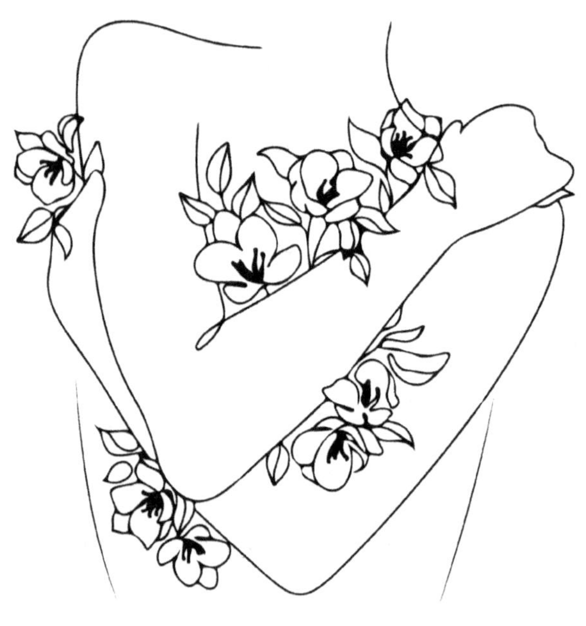

Body Positive

Scars are a reminder that you survived -
Fought a battle and won.
Your stomach is a reminder that you brought
life into this world,
A life that loves you beyond measure.
Your legs have carried you for years
And will continue to be strong.
Your hips are like handles,
Giving him something to hold on to.
Your body is beautiful.
It's the only one you have.
Take care of her.
Love her.
Love yourself.

Advice

Live your life for yourself.
Honor who you are.
Love yourself first and know your worth.
Love hard and love fast;
But love carefully.
Never compromise on what you need,
Because you deserve it, and more.
Listen to your gut the first time.
There are no do-overs.

Every Day is Poetry

The sun wakes me, whispers of light across my
face.
The blanket on my skin is a welcome reminder
of a new day.
My son, my light, brightens the day with kisses,
declarations of love, and stories from dreams he
doesn't remember.
I start the daily toil but am thankful for the air in
my lungs, and your good morning messages.
I go to work and remind myself of the positive.
Air in my lungs.
The movement in my body.
The reminders that I am here for a reason.
Every day is a reason to exist,
To be thankful,
To find the beauty in the day.
To find the poetry.

A Gallery of the Heart

My heart holds all the memories of my life,
Both good and bad.
Look inside and you'll see...
Pain
Anger
Hurt
Sadness
Home
Security
You
Him
Her
Food
Pets
Books
Grief

But, above all else, LOVE,

For it, for all.
But especially for you.

Touch

My skin turns to gooseflesh and
Chills run through my body
At the memory of your touch.
Your hands gripping my leg,
Teeth bruising my shoulder,
Lips grazing my neck,
Feeling your pleasure
In your strokes and your breath against my skin
and
In your eyes, as you look into mine.
I want to be engulfed in your touch
And have the daily reminders send shivers
through my body,
Anticipating the next.

Out of Sorts

I don't know how to act around you.
I get out of sorts.
Just the sight of you throws me off my rhythm,
But in the best of ways.
I get out of sorts.
My skin glows.
My cheeks puff up from the smile.
My eyes develop crow's feet,
But I love them because they're showing up for
the best reasons.
I get out of sorts.
I hold your hand,
Give you kisses,
Get my back rubbed. It's been so long,
I get out of sorts.
And I want to be out of sorts as long as I can.

Tears

Tears say so much.
Running the gamut of emotions
And telling stories that words otherwise cannot.
Tears aren't a weakness.
Tears are a strength.
There is strength in pain and vulnerability.
Salty rivulets running down your face
Serve as a reminder of what you've been
through.
Cry all the tears.
Feel cleansed and purified,
Then, pick yourself up
And start over.

Power

Recognizing your value
gives you more power
than you could imagine.
Don't let anyone tell you
what you're worth.
Only you determine that.
And your worth is immeasurable.

LOVE

Smiles, hugs, patience.
Passion, energy.
Warmth, joy.
Peace, togetherness.
Trust.

Silence

Silence so deep, you can hear the grass grow.
Leaves rustle gently
In pulses and waves.
The crunch of branches,
As small animals settle in for the night.
Birds making nests.
Deer taking one last graze.
Quiet rustling
As the wind gently blows through the grass.
The gentle sound of dew drops
Dripping from tree tops.
The woods breathe,
Even if we can't see it happen.

Passion

Uncontrollable emotions
Constantly running through my mind,
Unable to stop thinking about you.
Wishing I could be with you,
With your hand around my waist.
Rubbing my back.
Kissing me deeply.
My arms wrapped around you,
Pulling you closer,
And ending in bed,
A tangle of limbs and
Uncontrollable emotions.

Questions

Why me?
Was it fate or pure chance?
Did you like what you saw,
Or was it more?
Could you see my aura?
Or did you see the sadness in my photos?
Am I everything you expected?
Everything you wanted?
Do you want more?
Do you want all of me?
Do you dare to love me?

Twenty

Warm
Safe
Energized
Joyful
Lucky
Nurtured
Appreciated
Fulfilled
Beautiful
Protected
Peaceful
Authentic
Understood
Sexy
Desired
Attractive
Valued
Adventurous
Supported
Wonderful.

The list could go on.
20 words are just too few,
To tell you how you make me feel.

Loneliness

Loneliness is a funny thing.
You think you're ok with
Solitude.
But then someone comes along
Who you can't imagine
Being without.
That person
Who makes your heart race,
Puts a smile on your face,
And reminds you that
You weren't really lonely.
You just didn't have
The right person,
To cure you of loneliness.

Always On My Mind

From the moment I open my eyes
My thoughts fall on you.
How do you sleep?
Do you wish I was with you?
Do you think of me, the way I think of you?
The smallest of things
Bring you back to the forefront of my thoughts,
Sending random shivers through my body.
I think of you and wonder,
"How did I get so lucky?"
But that doesn't matter,
Because I'm happy.

Just Feel It

I don't think about what I'm going to write.
I just let the words flow from my brain
to my fingers,
to come out the tip of my pen.
I reflect and let the feelings of the day
Wash over me.
Happiness or sadness.
Anger or fear.
Any of them could emerge
But I tend not to put pen to paper
When my mood is sour.
Lately, my mood has been
Positive.
Affirmative.
Confident.
Loving.
And while my writing isn't perfect,
It's a start.
As long as I continue to feel,
I'll continue to write.

Anticipation

Waiting for you,
Your call,
Your message,
A picture,
A glimpse into your day.
Sometimes it's hard to focus
As I wait.
But when it comes,
My heart lifts open.
Do you think of me
As much as I think of you?
I hope so.
I hope you feel the same anticipation I feel
When we're apart.

Out of Order

Things feel out of order.
Unnatural,
Different,
Shaky.
But simultaneously,
Things feel perfect.
Like blocks that get put together incorrectly,
Yet create something of beauty.
Being out of order is subjective.
Who defined 'order'?
My order is whatever makes me happy.
And the disorder I feel
Makes me feel ordered.

Hope

The day I met you
My lost hope was found.
From that first interaction,
To that last kiss.
Hope was restored.
It sounds silly but,
Your manners,
Your smile,
The compliments,
Fun,
Conversations,
Jokes.
Your style.
The way you took control.
It all restored my hope
That I didn't have to be lonely.
You restored my hope
And my heart.

Heat

Warmth across my lips,
Sticky and wet
Like melted cotton candy,
Tequila shots in my chest,
Shivers up my spine.

9 789395 223058